MW01247473

Mountain Playgrounds of the Pike National Forest

MOUNTAIN PLAYGROUNDS
OF THE
PIKE NATIONAL FOREST

HIS MAJESTY—PIKES PEAK

Washington : : United States Department of Agriculture, Forest Service : : 1919

UNITED STATES DEPARTMENT OF AGRICULTURE

DEPARTMENT CIRCULAR 41

Contribution from the Forest Service

HENRY S. GRAVES, Forester

MOUNTAIN PLAYGROUNDS
══ OF THE ══
PIKE NATIONAL FOREST

A PLAYGROUND FOR THE NATION.

THE Pike National Forest, stretching for 80 miles along the eastern slope of the Continental Divide in Colorado, embraces one of the most popular recreation grounds in America. Within its boundaries is the greater part of the famous Pikes Peak region, visited annually by thousands of pleasure seekers, while in other portions of its more than 1,000,000 acres an exhilarating climate and the finest of mountain scenery combine to afford rare opportunities for health, rest, and enjoyment. Few other regions offer such varied attractions for the tourist, the camper, the nature lover, and all others who enjoy life in the open. More than 400,000 people visit the Pike National Forest each year.

That portion of the Rocky Mountains included in the Pike Forest was among the first to be explored by white men. It was visited by the early Spaniards, and after the famous expedition of Lieut. Zebulon M. Pike in 1806 was the goal of every traveler crossing the Great Plains. Tourists and health seekers began to visit the region in 1872, and ever since then its popularity as a pleasure ground has steadily increased.

From an economic standpoint the Pike National Forest is of the greatest importance, for it protects the water supply of a vast section of irrigated ranches and of many of Colorado's principal towns and cities, and contains a large store of timber for future local needs. Recognizing its value also as a great public playground, the Forest Service is doing everything possible to develop its recreational resources. Visitors may camp anywhere on Government land within the Forest boundaries and stay as long as they like. They may fish and hunt in the Forest, subject only to the Colorado fish and game laws. Forest officers are always ready to give pleasure seekers whatever information and assistance they can. All that is asked of visitors is to be careful with fire and to leave their camp sites clean.

In this booklet are described briefly some of the more prominent recreational features of the Pike National Forest. Detailed information can always be obtained at the headquarters of the Forest in the Majestic Building, Denver, or from local field officers.

CAMPING GROUNDS.

Along the many streams which head within the Pike Forest are any number of delightful camping places, together with an abundance of wood and pure water   A few of the most attractive are noted.

Mount Evans Playground. An increasing number of campers, fishermen, and mountain climbers are attracted each year to the Mount Evans region, which has been set aside by the Forest Service as a special summer playground   The area is of great scenic beauty, with rugged peaks towering above timber line, countless small lakes surrounded by precipitous cliffs, and an abundance of wild life. Mount Evans, the point of greatest interest, is 14,260 feet in elevation and is one of the three sentinel peaks in the Front Range of the Colorado Rockies   Bear Creek and its tributaries, together with Beartrack, Lost, Truesdale, and Roosevelt Lakes have been noted for years among fishermen as excellent trout waters   Deer, mountain sheep, ptarmigan, grouse, and numberless small creatures of fur and feather are found in these mountain lands

A road suitable for automobiles extends from Denver via Bear Creek and Evergreen to within 5 miles of this region.   From this point good Government trails lead into all parts of this great mountain playground   On the main trail to the summit of Mount Evans, two stopping places for travelers have been set aside and improved by the Forest Service   The first of these is the Beaver Meadows Camp Site, where shelter cabins, woods fireplaces, and a comfort station have been erected   A good spring has also been developed, and plenty of firewood is close at hand   At the Mount Evans Camp Site, a few miles below timber line, a substantial log cabin has been built and furnished in cooperation with the Colorado Mountain Club. This recreation cabin is open to visitors at all times.

North Fork of Clear Creek is reached from Denver by automobile in a three hours' run through the celebrated Denver Mountain Parks to Idaho Springs, and thence by the "Midland Trail."   Excellent

PILLARS OF HERCULES, SOUTH CHEYENNE CANYON, NEAR COLORADO SPRINGS
HEIGHT, 940 AND 740 FEET

camping sites may also be reached by wagon, distance 5 miles, from Empire on the Clear Creek Division of the Colorado & Southern Railway. Fishing is fairly good in upper Clear Creek, and there is a plentiful supply of pure water and firewood.

North Fork of South Platte River. This region is one of the greatest tourist resort centers in the Rocky Mountains A large part of the valley land is patented, but occasional camping sites are to be found along the river and near the small towns that dot the valley Fishing in the Platte is good, and supplies and mail facilities are close at hand. The "South Park Highway," from Denver via Morrison to South Park and Leadville, enters the North Fork Valley at Baileys (distance 47 miles), and continues up the river to Kenosha Pass The South Park Division of the Colorado & Southern Railway also runs the entire length of the valley

South Fork of South Platte River. The South Fork of the South Platte is the paramount fishing grounds of the Pike Forest, reached from Denver via the Colorado & Southern Railway to South Platte, and thence up river by automobile stage or wagon, or by automobile via the "South Platte Cut-Off" from Sedalia to Deckers Springs, distance 52 miles This region is also accessible from Colorado Springs via the "Pikes Peak Ocean to Ocean Highway" to Woodland Park, thence north through Manitou Park to West Creek and down the creek to Deckers, total distance 55 miles. The South Fork of the South Platte is well stocked with trout, and the scenery along the river is especially pleasing Camp sites abound, and firewood and good water are everywhere close at hand.

Chicago Lakes. The Chicago Lakes country, located on Chicago Creek directly under the north face of Mount Evans in what is locally known as the "Frying Pan Basin," is one of the most beautiful and spectacular camping spots in the northern part of the Pike Forest. The lakes, two in number, are set just above the dense Engelmann spruce forests of timber line, and are walled about on the south and west by stupendous cliffs rising sheer 2,000 feet from the water's edge, while along the north and east shores excellent camping sites are available. This lake region is 15 miles from Idaho Springs on the "Midland Trail" and Colorado & Southern Railway, and is accessible for about 10 miles by a fair mountain automobile road, the remainder of the trip to the lakes being made on horseback or on foot over a good trail   Excellent fishing is to be had in both lakes and also in Chicago Creek   From the main trail leading to the lakes a branch trail bears off to Echo Lake, Goliath Peak, Summit Lake, and Mount Evans.

Lost Park, situated along Lost Park Creek at an altitude of about 9,000 feet, is accessible by wagon or saddle horse and pack train from Jefferson, a station on the Colorado & Southern Railway some 20 miles distant   The trip requires about six hours   This park is surrounded by heavily timbered mountains which rise to elevations of from 10,000 to 11,500 feet   Mountain sheep, deer, and other wild game can often be seen.   Fishing is excellent, and the locality offers a most delightful camping ground for people who desire to get entirely away from towns and settlements

Jefferson Lake is about 7 miles by wagon road from the town of Jefferson.   It lies at an altitude of 10,500 feet in a basin surrounded by heavy timber and covers almost 250 acres   Fishing is generally good, and many large trout are caught in these waters

Other camp sites on the Pike Forest particularly easy of access are those along Rock Creek, south of Colorado Springs on the Canyon City auto road; in Waldo and Williams Canyons, within a mile of the town of Manitou, in the Manitou Park and West Creek country, 8 to 20 miles north of Woodland Park on the "Pikes Peak Ocean to Ocean Highway," and along Tarryall Creek to the north of Lake George. The canyons near Colorado Springs and Manitou are very popular with picnic parties and those who do not wish to outfit for a camping trip in the more remote regions   Four of the most popular picnic sites in Waldo Canyon have been improved by the Forest Service with woods fireplaces and comfort stations.

FISHING.

Within the boundaries of the Pike Forest are 250 miles of good fishing streams, teeming with eastern brook, black-speckled, and rainbow trout, besides many well-stocked lakes in which fish of large size may be caught.   Among the best fishing waters are the headwaters of the North and Middle Forks of Clear Creek, reached by automobile and the Clear Creek Division of the Colorado & Southern Railway; North and South Forks of the South Platte River and their tributaries, accessible by both automobile and the South Park Division of the Colorado & Southern Railway, Tarryall and Michigan Creeks in South Park, and Goose and Lost Park Creeks in the Tarryall country, reached from Jefferson on the same railroad, Turkey Creek, south of Lake Cheesman, reached by automobile from Florissant on the "Pikes Peak Ocean to Ocean Highway", Beaver Creek, south of Palmer Lake, on the main Denver–Colorado Springs automobile road, East, Middle, and West Beaver Creeks, south of Pikes Peak, reached by wagon road and train from Cripple Creek, and Catamount, Crystal, and French Creeks, to the north and east of Pikes Peak, accessible from the "Pikes Peak Ocean to Ocean Highway" and the Pikes Peak Auto Highway (toll road)

BIG-GAME AREAS.

The hunting of big game, other than certain species of predatory animals, is at present prohibited by the laws of Colorado in the hope that the State, once a favorite haunt of wild life, will again become the habitation of game animals Those who like to stalk their game with a camera, however, or those who wish to study the habits of wild life in its native haunts, will find much of interest in the Pike Forest

Bear are fairly plentiful in all parts of the Forest, and mountain sheep can be seen on the higher ranges which extend above timber line The big game area most easy of access is the north slope of Pikes Peak, where deer and mountain sheep may often be observed by a few hours' trip from Manitou, Colorado Springs, Cascade, and other near-by stations on the Midland Terminal Railway Fifty head of elk from Wyoming were turned loose in this vicinity in 1916, and other shipments have been liberated in the vicinity of Idaho Springs in the northern part of the Forest

Deer and mountain sheep are most numerous in the Mount Evans country, the Tarryall and Kenosha Ranges, and in the Platte Mountains region. Probably more than 2,000 deer and 800 mountain sheep have their home in the Pike Forest.

Visitors wishing to hunt and fish should inform themselves regarding open seasons, license requirements, and similar matters. Forest and local State officers can give this information

MOUNTAIN CLIMBING.

The Pike Forest offers exceptional opportunities for mountain climbing Within its boundaries are five peaks exceeding 14,000

ON THE TRAIL TO PIKES PEAK

feet in height, and more than 20 peaks over 11,000 feet. From many of these one is afforded a vast unobstructed view of mountains, foothills, and plains.

. Pikes Peak, elevation 14,109 feet, is the most popular climb, for this beacon of the Rockies is probably better known than any other mountain in America. The trip from Manitou to the summit on foot requires from 6 to 8 hours, and the return journey 3 hours. The peak may also be reached by cog road and automobile from Manitou and Colorado Springs.

Other noted peaks frequented by climbers are Mount Evans, 14,260 feet; Gray's and Torrey's Peaks, 14,341 and 14,336 feet, respectively; James Peak, 13,260 feet; and the Devil's Head, on which is located a Forest Service fire-lookout station.

FIRE PROTECTION AND CAMP SANITATION.

The Devil's Head lookout is the nucleus of the fire detection system of the Pike Forest. On this observation point, which overlooks a million acres of forest and plain, an officer is on constant watch

2444°—19——2

during the summer season for fire in the woods. When smoke is discovered, the Forest ranger nearest the fire is notified by telephone A fire on a National Forest is always fought until extinguished, no matter how long it takes

The watersheds of the Pike Forest are the sources of the streams upon which the cities, towns, and ranches of their plains, with a total population of over 400,000, depend for water for irrigation and domestic use. The protection of these forested areas from fire is therefore of the greatest importance, and fire detection and suppression takes precedence over all other work.

The greater percentage of the fires which occur in the mountains are due to human agencies, and are therefore preventable Visitors are urgently requested to be careful with fire when in the woods, and to cooperate with the Forest officers by reporting promptly any fires they may discover. Telephones are conveniently located in many parts of the Forest, and these may be used to call up the nearest officer in case a fire is seen

In order that the many attractive camp and picnic grounds of the Pike Forest may always be inviting to the public, they must be kept clean and sanitary Tin cans and camp refuse should be buried, and discarded clothing, papers, and other inflammable material burned A little thoughtfulness in this matter on the part of campers will do much toward increasing the pleasure of other visitors who follow.

RIVERS AND LAKES.

Among the streams in the Pike Forest which offer special scenic attractions are the North and South Forks of the South Platte River, with their rugged and towering rock walls; Clear Creek, emerging from the mountains through a beautiful canyon and then crossing the plains to form a junction with the South Platte near Denver, Fountain Creek, a tributary of the Arkansas, flowing through the famous Ute Pass, historic because of the fact that it was one of the main routes of travel for the Ute Indians many years prior to the advent of the white man, and North and South Cheyenne Canyons near Colorado Springs, famous for their unusual scenic beauty and wonderful waterfalls

More than 100 lakes, large and small, lie within the Pike Forest boundaries, principally at the foot of the Continental Divide The most important of these are Caroline, Chinn, Ice, Ohman, Reynolds, Sherwin, Slater, and Stuart Lakes, and Loch Lomond, on the headwaters of Fall River, northwest of Idaho Springs; the Chicago Lakes on Chicago Creek, southwest of the same town; Clear, Green, and Naylor Lakes, on South Clear Creek, above Georgetown; Duck, Beartrack, Lincoln, and Summit Lakes, and Lake Abyss, around Mount Evans; Jefferson Lake, near the town of Jefferson, in South Park; Wellington Lake, south of Buffalo on the North Fork of the South Platte; Lake Cheesman, the storage reservoir for the Denver city water supply, and Lake Moraine and Seven Lakes in the Pikes Peak region, which supply Colorado Springs and Manitou with water for domestic and municipal purposes.

WATERFALLS.

Among the more beautiful waterfalls in the Forest are the famous Seven Falls in South Cheyenne Canyon; St. Marys Falls, on a branch of North Cheyenne Creek, where the water descends over

A RANGER STATION IN THE PIKE NATIONAL FOREST, ON THE "PIKES PEAK OCEAN TO OCEAN HIGHWAY"

1,000 feet within a horizontal distance of about 200 feet, Silver Cascades and the Helen Hunt Falls, on the same stream, Green Mountain Falls, near the summer resort of that name, the series of falls in Cascade Creek, terminating just above the town of Cascade, in Ute Pass, Crystal Creek Falls, Ruxton Creek Falls, near the town of Manitou, Ruby Creek Falls, on a tributary of Little Bear Creek, in the Mount Evans region, where a silvery stream of water takes an abrupt drop of several hundred feet, and Elk Creek Falls.

GEOLOGICAL FORMATIONS.

Many unusual geological formations add interest to the Pike Forest region. Among these is the Tertiary Lake basin in the vicinity of Florissant, which contains numerous fossil beds where well-preserved specimens of plants, insects, birds, fish, and other forms of life of the Miocene period are embedded in volcanic shale. In this locality is also the famous petrified forest, one of the largest stumps of which has a diameter of 20 feet. The "Pikes Peak Ocean to Ocean Highway" passes through this lake basin, which may also be reached by stage from Divide on the Midland Terminal Railway running up Ute Pass, or by private automobile from Colorado Springs.

There are also interesting geological formations in Waldo and Williams Canyons, near Manitou, where the sandstone walls have been worn by the action of water and weather into fantastic shapes. The beautiful Queens Canyon along Camp Creek, in the same general locality, with its precipitous walls and many hidden caves, also is of considerable geologic interest

SUMMER HOME SITES.

Many people desire to spend a longer time on the National Forests than is represented by a trip of a few days or weeks. Under the act of Congress of March 4, 1915, sites for summer homes in the National Forests may be obtained for a term of years at a relatively small annual rental.

To meet the demands for summer-home sites in the Pike National Forest, 128 lots have been surveyed and plotted, and maps and information regarding them, together with photographs of the areas, are kept on file in the supervisor's office in Denver. These plots have been laid out only in such localities as are at present reasonably

WELLINGTON LAKE AND CASTLE PEAK

PICNICKERS INDULGING IN HOLIDAY SPORTS IN THE PIKE NATIONAL FOREST

accessible or have unusual scenic attractions and are otherwise desirable for summer-home purposes. They include sites on the South Platte River near the junction of the North and South Forks, and at various other places along the North Fork of this stream; in Waldo Canyon near Manitou; in South Cheyenne Canyon near Fairview; on Buffalo Creek in North Cheyenne Canyon; on Crystola Creek near Crystola, on the Midland Terminal Railway; in Blandin Gulch, about 5 miles south of Eldowe, on the same railroad; and on Little Fountain Creek below Cather Springs, on the old Colorado Springs–Cripple Creek stage road.

These are only a few of the many desirable summer-home sites on the Forest, and it is not intended in any way to limit the public to a choice from the plots already surveyed. Application for summer-home and kindred permits for any area on the Forest will be acted upon promptly. The existing surveys, however, will furnish considerable information in concrete form to prospective applicants concerning individual sites.

LAKE CHEESMAN, FROM WHICH DENVER OBTAINS ITS WATER SUPPLY

ACCOMMODATIONS FOR VISITORS IN AND NEAR THE FOREST.

A great number of hotels and summer resorts in and near the Pike Forest offer accommodation for those who visit the mountains. Among the resorts are: Cascade, in the famous Ute Pass, on the Midland Terminal Railway, at the junction of the Pikes Peak Auto Highway and the "Pikes Peak Ocean to Ocean Highway"; Green Mountain Falls and Woodland Park, also in Ute Pass, on the Midland Terminal Railway and the "Pikes Peak Ocean to Ocean Highway"; Glen Cove, just below timber line on the Pikes Peak Auto Highway; Half-Way House on the Pikes Peak "Cog Road"; "Camp Lavley" in beautiful North Cheyenne Canyon near Colorado Springs; Deckers Springs, and "The Wigwam," on the South Platte River, accessible by automobile from Denver and by daily auto stage from South Platte on the Colorado & Southern Railway; Buffalo Creek, on the North Fork of the South Platte near the mouth of the creek by that name; South

Platte, on the Colorado & Southern Railway at the junction of the North and South Forks of the South Platte; Wellington, on a beautiful lake by that name, accessible by automobile from Denver and from Buffalo Creek, on the Colorado & Southern Railway; and Strontia Springs, Longview, Foxton, Riverview, Bryn Mawr, Pine Grove, Estabrook, Insmont, Baileys, Glenisle, Grousemont, Shawnee, Singleton, and Cassells, all located on the Colorado & Southern Railway in the canyon of the North Fork of the South Platte River; Idaho Springs, Empire, and Georgetown on the Clear Creek Division of the Colorado & Southern Railway, and Glen Park and Pine Crest near Palmer Lake on the Denver & Rio Grande and Colorado & Southern Railroads and the "Colorado to Gulf Highway." Unlimited accommodations are also available at Denver, Colorado Springs, and Manitou.

OUTFITTING POINTS FOR TRIPS IN THE MOUNTAINS.

Denver, the gateway to the National Forests of Colorado, is the principal outfitting point for trips into the mountains, and almost any general locality in the Pike Forest can be reached from it in from 2 to 6 hours by rail. Colorado Springs also is a well-known outfitting point, particularly for the Pikes Peak region.

Other good outfitting points, where almost any articles needed for a trip into the Rockies may be purchased and livery and auto supplies secured, are Idaho Springs, Georgetown, Baileys, Manitou, Green Mountain Falls, Woodland Park, and Cripple Creek.

LINES OF TRAVEL.

The Pike Forest, with its four lines of railroads and two transcontinental highways running to all parts of the mountains, is the most accessible vacation ground in Colorado.

The Idaho Springs branch of the Colorado & Southern Railway extends along the Forest boundary in the Clear Creek Canyon region, ending with the famous Georgetown Loop at Silver Plume, from which town Grays and Torreys Peaks, 14,341 and 14,366 feet, respectively, as well as numerous other high mountains, are easily accessible. A branch of this line also runs from Forks Creek to the celebrated Central City mining district.

The South Park branch of the Colorado & Southern Railway crosses the Forest through Platte Canyon and over Kenosha Pass, making accessible the numerous summer resorts of this region, and continues westward through South Park and over Boreas Pass to Leadville.

The Manitou & Pikes Peak Railway ("Cog Road"), from Manitou to the summit of Pikes Peak, is operated during the summer season for the accommodation of tourists.

The Midland Terminal Railway, from Colorado Springs to Cripple Creek, ascends Ute Pass to Divide and thence turns south, following along that part of the Forest lying west of Pikes Peak.

The Sante Fe, Colorado & Southern, and Denver & Rio Grande Railroads also skirt the east boundary of the Pike Forest from Denver to Colorado Springs.

A great number of automobile roads take the visitor to many portions of the Forest. Some of the most noted highways are the boulevard over Lookout Mountain and through the Denver Mountain Parks to Idaho Springs and other points in Clear Creek Canyon, then crossing the Continental Divide over Berthoud Pass via the "Midland Trail"; the road up Bear Creek Canyon from Denver to the vicinity of Evergreen and Camp Rock; the "South Park Highway" up the North Fork of the South Platte via Morrison, Turkey Creek or Evergreen, and Baileys; the recently constructed Forest Service road from Sedalia to Deckers Springs, thence to West Creek and Lake George, where it joins the "Pikes Peak Ocean to Ocean Highway"; the "Pikes Peak Ocean to Ocean Highway," leading westward from Colorado Springs up Ute Pass; the Pikes Peak Auto Highway (toll road), a double-track auto road of standard construction from Cascade to the summit of Pikes Peak, and the "Colorado–Gulf Highway" along the Front Range boundary of the Forest from Denver southward.

Good wagon roads also run to all parts of the Forest, and there are practically no localities which can not be reached by trail.

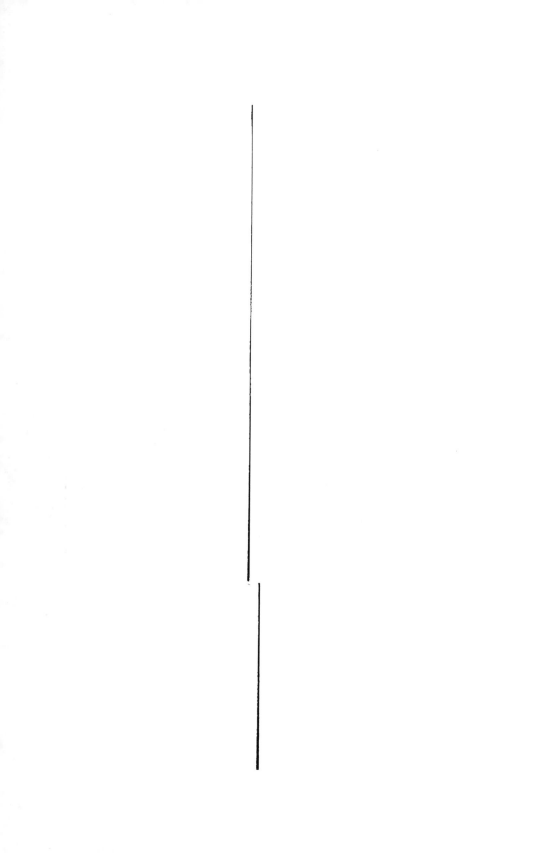

FOLDOUT BLANK

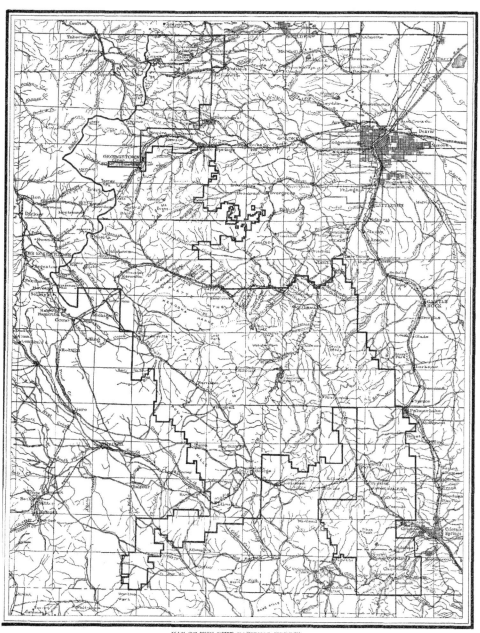

MAP OF THE PIKE NATIONAL FOREST

Solid black lines represent Forest boundaries.   Distances between solid light lines (township boundaries) represent 6 miles

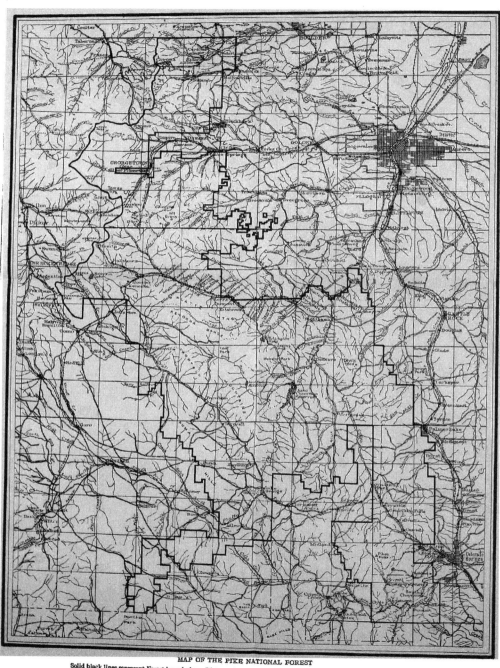

MAP OF THE PIKE NATIONAL FOREST

Solid black lines represent Forest boundaries.   Distances between solid light lines (township boundaries) represent 6 miles

CPSIA information can be obtained
at www.ICGtesting.com
Printed in the USA
BVHW040930200221
600354BV00018B/460

9 781374 513761